MW01139309

Three Stories of CHRISTMAS

Three Stories of CHRISTMAS

Mary's Christmas Story
The Shepherd's Christmas
Three Presents For Baby Jesus

An ARCH BOOKS® Gift Collection

An Inspirational Press Book
for Children

First Inspirational Press edition published in 2000.

Inspirational Press
A division of BBS Publishing Corporation
386 Park Avenue South
New York, NY 10016

Inspirational Press is a registered trademark of BBS Publishing Corporation.

Published by arrangement with Concordia Publishing House.

Library of Congress Control Number: 00-134227

ISBN: 0-88486-261-5

Printed in Mexico

Mary's Christmas Story

Luke 1:26–56
Luke 2:1–20 for children

Written by Teresa Olive
Illustrated by Nancy Munger

Young Mary lived in Nazareth, a town in Galilee.
She was a girl who tried to serve the Lord most faithfully.
As Mary sat quietly in her home one night,
The angel Gabriel appeared, shining oh so bright!

"Greetings!" said Gabriel. "You're favored by the Lord!"
Mary felt afraid and trembled at his words.
But the angel gently said, "Mary, do not fear.
God is very pleased with you, and He sent me here.

"You will have a baby named Jesus, God's own Son.
He will sit on David's throne, ruling everyone."
Mary did not understand. She asked, "How can this be?
I am still a virgin. I'm not married yet, you see."

Gabriel said, "God Himself will cause you to conceive.
Nothing is impossible with God—you may believe!
Your relative, Elizabeth, who is old and worn,
Is finally a mother—her child will soon be born."

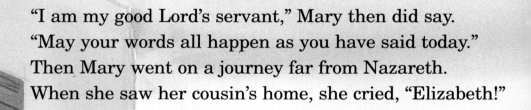

"I am my good Lord's servant," Mary then did say.
"May your words all happen as you have said today."
Then Mary went on a journey far from Nazareth.
When she saw her cousin's home, she cried, "Elizabeth!"

As Mary spoke, Elizabeth felt her baby boy
Leaping high within her womb, jumping up with joy!
Elizabeth knew right away that Mary was the one
God had chosen as the mother of His only Son.

Mary said, "The Mighty One has been so good to me,
And to all of Israel—He's come to set us free!"
Mary stayed there visiting until three months were gone.
Then Elizabeth gave birth to a son named John.

And then King Caesar issued this command:
"A census will be taken throughout all the land."
So Mary and Joseph had to pack and travel down
To Bethlehem, since it was Joseph's family's town.

When at last they arrived in tiny Bethlehem,
Every room was full—there was no room for them.
Finally, an innkeeper invited them to stay
In his barn where they could sleep on the oxen's hay.

Soon the time came for the baby to be born.
Mary swaddled Him in cloths so He was snug and warm.
There was no crib or cradle for baby Jesus' bed,
So Mary gently laid Him on the manger's hay instead.

As Mary gazed upon the face of her newborn Son,
Some shepherds came in saying, "He must be the one!"
Then they told their story: "We were watching sheep.
It was dark and quiet. We were half asleep.

"Suddenly, we saw a sight that jolted us awake—
An angel so glorious, our knees began to shake!
We fell down upon the ground, trembling in fear.
The angel said, 'Don't be afraid. I bring news of good
      cheer!

"'In the town of Bethlehem, God's Son was born today.
You will find Him wrapped in cloths in a manger's hay.'
Next we saw a host of angels lighting up the sky,
Lifting up their voices to the Lord Most High.

"They said, 'Glory to the Lord! Peace on earth to men!'
Then the angels vanished. It was dark again.
At first, we all just stood there, then we began to shout,
'Let us go to see the child the Lord told us about!'

"So we ran here and found it all just as the angel said—
Here's the Baby wrapped in cloths in His manger bed!"
Then the shepherds went around, telling everyone,
"God has sent a Savior—Jesus, His own Son!"

The people were amazed in crowded Bethlehem.
Could this baby be the King God had promised them?
Mary treasured all of this deep within her heart,
Thanking God for using her for such a loving part.

Dear Parents:

She was young, poor, and powerless. So why did God choose Mary to be the mother of His Son? Precisely because she was young, poor, and powerless, just as we are powerless in the face of sin and death. God worked through a humble young girl, a bewildered carpenter, a powerful Roman ruler, and many others to accomplish His plan of sending His Son to be our Savior.

Explain to your child that God continues to work through His people today, using us to share His love with others. Keep Christ's birthday foremost in your Christmas celebration this year. Purchase or make an Advent calendar or an Advent wreath. Ask God each day to prepare your hearts to celebrate the birth of His Son. Say a special prayer, or act out the Christmas story before opening your presents. Draft family pets to play the parts of animals in the stable!

Take some pictures of your special activities and keep them in a photo album. Look at them often with your child. "Ponder" God's goodness as Mary did and thank Him for His great love in sending His Son to be our Savior.

The Editor

The Shepherd's Christmas

Luke 2:1–20 for Children

Written by Beth Atchison
Illustrated by Susan Morris

Night had come on shepherds' hill.
The sheep lay down to rest.
The shepherds smiled at one small lad
And teased in gentle jest.

"A little shepherd's first night watch
Could be a scary thing.
You might see bears in every bush.
You'd better bring your sling."

"I'm not afraid," the young boy said.
"I'm strong and brave and big."
But deep inside his heart would pound
At every snapping twig.

Then suddenly like lightning flash,
A bright light filled the sky.
And heaven opened wide as God
Sent an angel from on high.

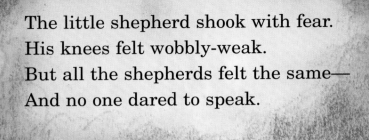

The little shepherd shook with fear.
His knees felt wobbly-weak.
But all the shepherds felt the same—
And no one dared to speak.

The angel said with joyful voice,
"There is no need to fear.
The Savior of the world is born,
And He is very near.

"We give all glory to our God.
This special night we sing!
Go quickly, now, and worship Him,
For He will be your King."

The little shepherd and the men
With haste went on their way.
The trembling boy felt most afraid.
What would he do or say?

They found Him—Jesus—in the straw,
A manger for a bed,
Within the stable in Bethlehem—
Just as the angel said.

The shepherds crowded all around
To see the baby's face,
Amazed to meet a little King
In this most humble place.

Jesus' face seemed full of peace
As He lay resting there,
Trusting in His Father's love
And in His parents' care.

Now the boy was not so scared
Inside the stable dim.
He would be braver for the King
Who would be brave for him.

The shepherds knelt down on the straw.
They worshiped Jesus there.
And when they left, they spread the news
To others everywhere.

From that time on the boy would watch
The sheep 'neath darkened sky.
And even when he was afraid,
He knew Christ was nearby.

So when you feel afraid of things,
Think of shepherds long ago
Who found peace in the promised King
And worshiped Him with joy.

For Jesus Christ is still the King
Who sits on heaven's throne.
He'll help you when you are afraid.
You'll never be alone.

Dear Parents:

We used a fictional shepherd boy in this story to help young children understand the awe and excitement of our Savior's birth. Explain to your child that, while storybooks sometimes present pretend characters, God's Word is always true. Read the Christmas story from Luke 2 to your child. Help your child manipulate the pieces in your crèche to act out the story.

Explain to your child that Jesus came to earth to live a perfect life for us and then give His life on the cross to take the punishment for our sins. Now He watches over us, continuing to love us, protect us, and hold us in safekeeping. Pray together, thanking Jesus for being our Savior and King.

The Editor

THREE PRESENTS FOR BABY JESUS

Matthew 2:1–12 for children

Written by Joanne Bader
Illustrated by Corbin Hillam

Far to the east of Bethlehem
The Wise Men studied stars.
Theirs was a dry and sandy land
With palm trees and bazaars.

One night they saw a brand-new star,
So high up in the sky.
It seemed much brighter than the rest.
They had to find out why.

They'd read about a certain star.
This star would be the thing
For them to follow so they'd see
Their Savior and their King.

"Let's pack our gifts and go right now.
The star will be our lead.
We'll have a chance to worship Him,"
One said, and all agreed.

The desert sand was hot and dry;
The camels' hooves dug deep.
They traveled many days and nights
With very little sleep.

They headed to Jerusalem,
For there they thought they'd see
The Son of God that had been born
So people would be free.

King Herod's home was where they stopped
To ask a favor there,
"Please help us find the baby King
So we can kneel in prayer."

The smartest teachers and the priests
Were summoned to the court.
"The prophets have foretold His birth,"
They said in their report.

"The land of Judah, that's His home,
The city's Bethlehem."
The Magi then knew where to go
And said, "Thank you," to them.

King Herod was not pleased with this;
He did not like the news.
He did not want another king—
Who would the people choose?

He called the Wise Men back to him,
"Tell me where He is found
So I can come and worship Him
And spread the word around."

The bright star led them once again.
It stopped above the place
Where they could see God's own dear Son,
They'd see Him face to face.

His mother, Mary, held Him close.
They fell down on their knees.
They worshiped Him with joyful hearts,
The newborn King to please.

They brought their precious gifts to Him,
Some incense, myrrh, and gold.
They were so happy to be there,
For they had been so bold.

Before they went back home again,
God told them in a dream,
"Do not tell Herod where you've been,
He has an evil scheme."

They went back home another way
So Herod would not know.
Their faces showed their happiness,
Their hearts were all aglow.

Dear Parents:

This narrative from Matthew's gospel tells a special part of the Christmas story. The Wise Men were Gentiles from a foreign land, but they wanted to see Jesus, the King of the Jews. They traveled a great distance to worship Him and give Him their gifts.

This account reminds us of several important truths. Jesus came to earth to be the Savior of people of every race, color, and nationality. The Wise Men gave the most precious gifts they had to Jesus, reminding us of the precious gift of our salvation.

Celebrate God's wonderful gift of His Son with your child as you talk about the story of the Wise Men.

The Editor